DOVER·THRIFT·EDITIONS

Bacchae

EURIPIDES

DOVER PUBLICATIONS, INC.
Mineola, New York

DOVER THRIFT EDITIONS

GENERAL EDITOR: STANLEY APPELBAUM

Copyright

Published in Canada by General Publishing Company, Ltd., 30 Lesmill Road, Don Mills, Toronto, Ontario.

Bibliographical Note

This Dover edition, first published in 1997, is an unabridged, unaltered republication of the work translated by Henry Hart Milman as *The Bacchanals*, in *The Plays of Euripides*, volume two, originally published in 1908 by J. M. Dent, London, as part of Everyman's Library. (Milman's translation was first published in 1865.) A new Note has been written specially for the Dover edition.

Library of Congress Cataloging-in-Publication Data

Euripides.
    [Bacchae. English]
    Bacchae / Euripides.
        p.   cm. — (Dover thrift editions)
    "An unabridged, unaltered republication of the work translated by Henry Hart Milman . . . originally published in 1908" — T.p. verso.
    ISBN 0-486-29580-X (pbk.)
    1. Pentheus (Greek mythology) — Drama. 2. Dionysus (Greek deity) — Drama. 3. Bacchantes — Drama. I. Milman, Henry Hart, 1791–1868. II. Title. III. Series.
PA3975.B2M55   1997
882'.01 — dc21
                                             96-40062
                                               CIP

Manufactured in the United States of America
Dover Publications, Inc., 31 East 2nd Street, Mineola, N.Y. 11501

Note

THE YOUNGEST OF the three great Greek dramatists, Euripides (ca. 485 to ca. 406 B.C.) is represented by the largest number of extant plays (19, as compared with seven each for Aeschylus and Sophocles). He is, in the opinion of many scholars, the cruelest of the three in his view of the indifference or vindictiveness of the gods. Certainly, the *Bacchae* demonstrates this bleak outlook in the horrible vengeance Bacchus wreaks on Pentheus.

The legend as related in the play has a historic basis. The cult of Dionysus (Bacchus), who represents aspects of fruitfulness and regeneration, probably originated in Thrace and/or Phrygia. Wearing fawn skins and carrying the thyrsus (a staff topped by a pinecone or bunch of grapes and ivy), bacchants would work themselves into a frenzy (possibly drug-induced), issuing the cry "Evoë!" Observance of these rituals could also include *omophagia*, the rending of a sacrificial victim, usually a goat, limb from limb and subsequent consumption of the animal raw. Although the Bacchic rites observed in Greece were not as violent as those in Asia Minor, the cult met with strong male opposition and attempted suppression. Furthermore, the festivals at which dramas were presented constituted part of the rite of Dionysus, the term *tragoidia* (goat song), from which the word tragedy is derived, probably referring to the sacrificial goat.

But the *Bacchae* is not an anthropological study. It is an examination of a problem that weighed heavily on the Greek mind: the conflict of passion and reason and the necessity of striking a balance between the two.

Dramatis Personae

Dionysus

Chorus of Bacchae

Tiresias

Cadmus

Pentheus

Attendant

Messenger

Second Messenger

Agave

DIONYSUS   Unto this land of Thebes I come, Jove's son,
Dionysus; he whom Semele of yore,
'Mid the dread midwifery of lightning fire,
Bore, Cadmus' daughter. In a mortal form,
The God put off, by Dirce's stream I stand,
And cool Ismenos' waters; and survey
My mother's grave, the thunder-slain, the ruins
Still smouldering of that old ancestral palace,
The flame still living of the lightning fire,
Here's immortal vengeance 'gainst my mother.

And well hath reverent Cadmus set his ban
On that heaven-stricken, unapproached place,
His daughter's tomb, which I have mantled o'er
With the pale verdure of the trailing vine.

And I have left the golden Lydian shores,
The Phrygian and the Persian sun-seared plains,
And Bactria's walls; the Medes' wild wintry land
Have passed, and Araby the Blest; and all
Of Asia, that along the salt-sea coast
Lifts up her high-towered cities, where the Greeks,
With the Barbarians mingled, dwell in peace.

And everywhere my sacred choirs, mine Orgies
Have founded, by mankind confessed a God.
Now first in an Hellenic town I stand.

Of all the Hellenic land here first in Thebes,
I have raised my revel shout, my fawn-skin donned,

1

Ta'en in my hand my thyrsus, ivy-crowned.
        But here, where least beseemed, my mother's sisters
Vowed Dionysus was no son of Jove:
That Semele, by mortal paramour won,
Belied great Jove as author of her sin;
'Twas but old Cadmus' craft: hence Jove in wrath
Struck dead the bold usurper of his bed.
        So from their homes I've goaded them in frenzy;
Their wits all crazed, they wander o'er the mountains
And I have forced them wear my wild attire.
There's not a woman of old Cadmus' race,
But I have maddened from her quiet house;
Unseemly mingled with the sons of Thebes,
On the roofless rocks, 'neath the pale pines, they sit.
        Needs must this proud recusant city learn,
In our dread Mysteries initiate,
Her guilt, and humbly seek to make atonement
To me, for Semele, mine outraged mother —
To me, the God confessed, of Jove begot.
        Old Cadmus now his might and kingly rule
To Pentheus hath given up, his sister's son,
My godhead's foe; who from the rich libation
Repels me, nor makes mention of my name
In holy prayer. Wherefore to him, to Thebes,
And all her sons, soon will I terribly show
That I am born a God: and so depart
(Here all things well disposed) to other lands,
Making dread revelation of myself.
        But if this Theban city, in her ire,
With arms shall seek to drive from off the mountains
My Bacchanal rout, at my wild Mænads' head

I'll meet, and mingle in the awful war.
Hence have I ta'en the likeness of a man,
Myself transmuted into human form.
　　But ye, who Tmolus, Lydia's strength, have left
My Thyasus of women, whom I have led
From lands barbarian, mine associates here,
And fellow-pilgrims; lift ye up your drums,
Familiar in your native Phrygian cities,
Made by your mother Rhea's craft and mine;
And beat them all round Pentheus' royal palace,
Beat, till the city of Cadmus throngs to see.
I to the Bacchanals in the dim glens
Of wild Cithæron go to lead the dance.

CHORUS　From the Asian shore,
　　　　And by the sacred steep of Tmolus hoar,
　　　　Light I danced with wing-like feet,
　　　　Toilless toil and labour sweet!
　　　　Away! away! whoe'er he be;
　　　　Leave our path, our temple free!
　　　　Seal up each silent lip in holy awe.
　　　　But I, obedient to thy law,
　　O Dionysus! chant the choral hymn to thee

　　　　Blest above all of human line,
　　　　Who, deep in mystic rites divine,
　　　　Leads his hallowed life with us,
　　　　Initiate in our Thyasus;
　　　　And, purified with holiest waters,
　　Goes dancing o'er the hills with Bacchus' daughters.
　　　　And thy dark orgies hallows he,
　　　　O mighty mother, Cybele!

He his thyrsus shaking round,
All his locks with ivy crowned,
O Dionysus! boasts of thy dread train to be.

Bacchanals! away, away!
Lead your God in fleet array;
Bacchus lead, the ever young,
A God himself from Gods that sprung,
From the Phrygian mountains down
Through every wide-squared Grecian town.
Him the Theban queen of yore
'Mid Jove's fast-flashing lightnings bore:
In her awful travail wild
Sprung from her womb the untimely child,
While smitten with the thunderblast
The sad mother breathed her last.

Instant him Saturnian Jove
Received with all a mother's love;
In his secret thigh immured,
There with golden clasps secured,
Safe from Herè's jealous sight;
Then, as the Fates fulfilled, to light
He gave the hornéd god, and wound
The living snakes his brows around;
Whence still the wandéd Mænads bear
Their serpent prey wreathed in their floating hair.

Put on thy ivy crown,
O Thebes, thou sacred town!
O hallowed house of dark-haired Semele!

Bloom, blossom everywhere,
With flowers and fruitage fair,
And let your frenzied steps supported be
With thyrsi from the oak
Or the green ash-tree broke:
Your spotted fawn-skins line with locks
Torn from the snowy fleecéd flocks:
Shaking his wanton wand let each advance,
And all the land shall madden with the dance.

Bromius, that his revel rout
To the mountains leads about;
To the mountains leads along,
Where awaits the female throng;
From the distaff, from the loom,
Raging with the God they come.
O ye mountains, wild and high,
Where the old Kouretæ lie:
Glens of Crete, where Jove was nurst,
In your sunless caverns first
The crested Korybantes found
The leathern drums mysterious round,
That, mingling in harmonious strife
With the sweet-breathed Phrygian fife,
In Mother Rhea's hands they place,
Meet the Bacchic song to grace.
And the frantic Satyrs round
That ancient Goddess leap and bound:
And soon the Trieteric dances light
Began, immortal Bacchus' chief delight.

On the mountains wild 'tis sweet
When faint with rapid dance our feet;
Our limbs on earth all careless thrown
With the sacred fawn-skins strewn,
To quaff the goat's delicious blood,
A strange, a rich, a savage food.
Then off again the revel goes
O'er Phrygian, Lydian mountain brows;
Evoë! Evoë! leads the road,
Bacchus self the maddening God!
And flows with milk the plain, and flows with wine
Flows with the wild bees' nectar-dews divine;
And soars, like smoke, the Syrian incense pale —
The while the frantic Bacchanal
The beaconing pine-torch on her wand
Whirls around with rapid hand,
And drives the wandering dance about,
Beating time with joyous shout,
And casts upon the breezy air
All her rich luxuriant hair;
Ever the burthen of her song,
"Raging, maddening, haste along
Bacchus' daughters, ye the pride
Of golden Tmolus' fabled side;
While your heavy cymbals ring,
Still your 'Evoë! Evoë!' sing!"
Evoë! the Evian god rejoices
In Phrygian tones and Phrygian voices,
When the soft holy pipe is breathing sweet,
In notes harmonious to her feet,
Who to the mountain, to the mountain speeds;

Like some young colt that by its mother feeds,
   Gladsome with many a frisking bound,
The Bacchanal goes forth and treads the echoing ground.

TIRESIAS Ho! some one in the gates, call from his place
        Cadmus, Agenor's son, who, Sidon's walls
        Leaving, built up this towered city of Thebes.
        Ho! some one say, "Tiresias awaits him."
        Well knows he why I am here; the covenant
        Which I, th' old man, have made with him still older,
        To lift the thyrsus wand, the fawn-skin wear,
        And crown our grey hairs with the ivy leaves.

CADMUS Best friend! with what delight within my palace
        I heard thy speech, the speech of a wise man!
        Lo! I am here, in the God's sacred garb;
        For needs must we, the son of mine own daughter,
        Dionysus, now 'mongst men a manifest God,
        Even to the utmost of our power extol.
        Where shall we lead the dance, plant the light foot,
        And shake the hoary locks? Tiresias, thou
        The aged lead the aged: wise art thou,
        Nor will I weary night and day the earth
        Beating with my lithe thyrsus. Oh, how sweetly
        Will we forget we are old!

TIRESIAS   Thou'rt as myself:
        I too grow young; I too essay the dance.

CADMUS Shall we, then, in our chariots seek the mountains?

TIRESIAS It were not the same homage to the God.

CADMUS   The old man still shall be the old man's tutor.

TIRESIAS   The God will guide us thither without toil.

CADMUS   Of all the land, join we alone the dance?

TIRESIAS   All else misjudge; we only are the wise.

CADMUS   Too long we linger; hold thou fast mine hand.

TIRESIAS   Lo! thus true yoke-fellows join hand with hand.

CADMUS   I, mortal-born, may not despise the Gods.

TIRESIAS   No wile, no paltering with the deities.
        The ancestral faith, coeval with our race,
        No subtle reasoning, if it soar aloft
        Even to the height of wisdom, can o'erthrow.
        Some one will say that I disgrace mine age,
        Rapt in the dance, and ivy-crowned my head.
        The Gods admit no difference: old or young,
        All it behoves to mingle in the rite.
        From all he will receive the common honour,
        Nor deign to count his countless votaries.

CADMUS   Since thou, Tiresias, seest not day's sweet light,
        I, as thy Seer, must tell thee what is coming.
        Lo, Pentheus, hurrying homewards to his palace,
        Echion's son, to whom I have given the kingdom.
        He is strangely moved! What new thing will he say?

PENTHEUS   I have been absent from this land, and hear
        Of strange and evil doings in the city.
        Our women all have left their homes, to join

These fabled mysteries. On the shadowy rocks
Frequent they sit, this God of yesterday,
Dionysus, whosoe'er he be, with revels
Dishonourable honouring. In the midst
Stand the crowned goblets; and each stealing forth,
This way and that, creeps to a lawless bed;
In pretext, holy sacrificing Mænads,
But serving Aphrodite more than Bacchus.
All whom I've apprehended, in their gyves
Our officers guard in the public prison.
Those that have 'scaped I'll hunt from off the moun-
    tains,
Ino, Agave who to Echion bare me,
Her too, Autonoe, Antæus' mother;
And fettering them all in iron bonds,
I'll put an end to their mad wickedness.
'Tis said a stranger hath appeared among us,
A wizard, sorcerer, from the land of Lydia,
Beauteous with golden locks and purple cheeks,
Eyes moist with Aphrodite's melting fire.
And day and night he is with the throng, to guile
Young maidens to the soft inebriate rites.
    But if I catch him 'neath this roof, I'll silence
The beating of his thyrsus, stay his locks'
Wild tossing, from his body severing his neck.
He, say they, is the new God, Dionysus,
That was sewn up within the thigh of Jove.
He, with his mother, guiltily that boasted
Herself Jove's bride, was blasted by the lightning.
Are not such deeds deserving the base halter?
Sin heaped on sin! whoe'er this stranger be.

But lo, new wonders! see I not Tiresias,
The prophet, in the dappled fawn-skin clad?
My mother's father too (a sight for laughter!)
Tossing his hair? My sire, I blush for thee
Beholding thine old age thus fatuous grown.
Wilt not shake off that ivy? free thine hand
From that unseemly wand, my mother's father!
This is thy work, Tiresias. This new God
Wilt thou instal 'mongst men, at higher price
To vend new auspices, and well paid offerings.
If thine old age were not thy safeguard, thou
Shouldst pine in chains among the Bacchanal women.
False teacher of new rites! For where 'mong women
The grape's sweet poison mingles with the feast,
Nought holy may we augur of such worship.

CHORUS   Oh impious! dost thou not revere the Gods,
Nor Cadmus, who the earth-born harvest sowed?
Echion's son! how dost thou shame thy lineage!

TIRESIAS   'Tis easy to be eloquent, for him
That's skilled in speech, and hath a stirring theme.
Thou hast the flowing tongue as of a wise man,
But there's no wisdom in thy fluent words;
For the bold demagogue, powerful in speech,
Is but a dangerous citizen lacking sense.
This the new deity thou laugh'st to scorn,
I may not say how mighty he will be
Throughout all Hellas. Youth! there are two things
Man's primal need, Demeter, the boon Goddess
(Or rather will ye call her Mother Earth?),
With solid food maintains the race of man.

He, on the other hand, the son of Semele,
Found out the grape's rich juice, and taught us mortals
That which beguiles the miserable of mankind
Of sorrow, when they quaff the vine's rich stream.
Sleep too, and drowsy oblivion of care
He gives, all-healing medicine of our woes.
He 'mong the gods is worshipped a great god,
Author confessed to man of such rich blessings
Him dost thou love to scorn, as in Jove's thigh
Sewn up. This truth profound will I unfold:
When Jove had snatched him from the lightning-fire
He to Olympus bore the new-born babe.
Stern Herè strove to thrust him out of heaven,
But Jove encountered her with wiles divine:
He clove off part of th' earth-encircling air,
There Dionysus placed the pleasing hostage,
Aloof from jealous Herè. So men said
Hereafter he was cradled in Jove's thigh
(From the assonance of words in our old tongue
For thigh and hostage the wild fable grew).
A prophet is our god, for Bacchanalism
And madness are alike prophetical.
And when the god comes down in all his power,
He makes the mad to rave of things to come.
Of Ares he hath attributes: he the host
In all its firm array and serried arms,
With panic fear scatters, ere lance cross lance:
From Dionysus springs this frenzy too.
    And him shall we behold on Delphi's crags
Leaping, with his pine torches lighting up
The rifts of the twin-headed rock; and shouting

And shaking all around his Bacchic wand
Great through all Hellas. Pentheus, be advised!
Vaunt not thy power o'er man, even if thou thinkest
That thou art wise (it is diseased, thy thought),
Think it not! In the land receive the god.
Pour wine, and join the dance, and crown thy brows.
Dionysus does not force our modest matrons
To the soft Cyprian rites; the chaste by nature
Are not so cheated of their chastity.
Think well of this, for in the Bacchic choir
The holy woman will not be less holy.
Thou'rt proud, when men to greet thee throng the gates,
And the glad city welcomes Pentheus' name;
He too, I ween, delights in being honoured.
   I, therefore, and old Cadmus whom thou mock'st,
Will crown our heads with ivy, dance along
An hoary pair — for dance perforce we must;
I war not with the gods. Follow my counsel; ·
Thou'rt at the height of madness, there's no medicine
Can minister to disease so deep as thine.

CHORUS Old man! thou sham'st not Phœbus thine own god.
        Wise art thou worshipping that great god Bromius.

CADMUS My son! Tiresias well hath counselled thee;
        Dwell safe with us within the pale of law.
        Now thou fliest high: thy sense is void of sense.
        Even if, as thou declar'st, he were no god,
        Call thou him god. It were a splendid falsehood
        If Semele be thought t' have borne a god;
        'Twere honour unto us and to our race.
        Hast thou not seen Actæon's wretched fate?

The dogs he bred, who fed from his own board,
Rent him in wrath to pieces; for he vaunted
Than Artemis to be a mightier hunter.
So do not thou: come, let me crown thine head
With ivy, and with us adore the god.

PENTHEUS   Hold off thine hand! Away! Go rave and dance,
And wipe not off thy folly upon me.
On him, thy folly's teacher, I will wreak
Instant relentless justice. Some one go,
The seats from which he spies the flight of birds —
False augur — with the iron forks o'erthrow,
Scattering in wild confusion all abroad,
And cast his chaplets to the winds and storms;
Thou'lt gall him thus, gall to the height of bitterness.
Ye to the city! seek that stranger out,
That womanly man, who with this new disease
Afflicts our matrons, and defiles their beds:
Seize him and bring him hither straight in chains,
That he may suffer stoning, that dread death.
Such be his woful orgies here in Thebes.

TIRESIAS   Oh, miserable! That know'st not what thou sayest,
Crazed wert thou, now thou'rt at the height of madness:
But go we, Cadmus, and pour forth our prayer,
Even for this savage and ungodly man,
And for our city, lest the god o'ertake us
With some strange vengeance.
                              Come with thy ivy staff,
Lean thou on me, and I will lean on thee:
'Twere sad for two old men to fall, yet go
We must, and serve great Bacchus, son of Jove.

What woe, O Cadmus, will this woe-named man
Bring to thine house! I speak not now as prophet,
But a plain simple fact: fools still speak folly.

CHORUS   Holy goddess! Goddess old!
           Holy! thou the crown of gold
           In the nether realm that wearest,
           Pentheus' awful speech thou hearest,
           Hearest his insulting tone
           'Gainst Semele's immortal son,
           Bromius, of gods the first and best.
           At every gay and flower-crowned feast,
           His the dance's jocund strife,
           And the laughter with the fife,
           Every care and grief to lull,
           When the sparkling wine-cup full
           Crowns the gods' banquets, or lets fall
     Sweet sleep on the eyes of men at mortal festival.
           Of tongue unbridled without awe,
           Of madness spurning holy law,
           Sorrow is the Jove-doomed close;
           But the life of calm repose
           And modest reverence holds her state
           Unbroken by disturbing fate;
           And knits whole houses in the tie
           Of sweet domestic harmony.
           Beyond the range of mortal eyes
           'Tis not wisdom to be wise.
           Life is brief, the present clasp,
           Nor after some bright future grasp.
           Such were the wisdom, as I ween,

Only of frantic and ill-counselled men.

Oh, would to Cyprus I might roam,
    Soft Aphrodite's isle,
Where the young loves have their perennial home,
    That soothe men's hearts with tender guile:
Or to that wondrous shore where ever
The hundred-mouthed barbaric river
Makes teem with wealth the showerless land!
O lead me! lead me, till I stand,
Bromius! — sweet Bromius! — where high swelling
Soars the Pierian muses' dwelling —
Olympus' summit hoar and high —
Thou revel-loving deity!
    For there are all the graces,
        And sweet desire is there,
        And to those hallowed places
    To lawful rites the Bacchanals repair.
    The deity, the son of Jove,
        The banquet is his joy,
    Peace, the wealth-giver, doth he love,
        That nurse of many a noble boy.
    Not the rich man's sole possessing;
    To the poor the painless blessing
    Gives he of the wine-cup bright.
    Him he hates, who day and night,
    Gentle night, and gladsome day,
    Cares not thus to while away.
    Be thou wisely unsevere!
    Shun the stern and the austere!
        Follow the multitude;

Their usage still pursue!
Their homely wisdom rude
(Such is my sentence) is both right and true.

OFFICER Pentheus, we are here! In vain we went not forth:
The prey which thou commandest we have taken.
Gentle our quarry met us, nor turned back
His foot in flight, but held out both his hands;
Became not pale, changed not his ruddy colour.
Smiling he bade us bind, and lead him off,
Stood still, and made our work a work of ease.
Reverent I said, "Stranger, I arrest thee not
Of mine own will, but by the king's command."
But all the Bacchanals, whom thou hast seized
And bound in chains within the public prison,
All now have disappeared, released they are leaping
In their wild orgies, hymning the god Bacchus.
Spontaneous fell the chains from off their feet;
The bolts drew back untouched by mortal hand.
In truth this man, with many wonders rife
Comes to our Thebes. 'Tis thine t' ordain the rest.

PENTHEUS   Bind fast his hands! Thus in his manacles
Sharp must he be indeed to 'scape us now.
There's beauty, stranger — woman-witching beauty
(Therefore thou art in Thebes) — in thy soft form;
Thy fine bright hair, not coarse like the hard athlete's,
Is mantling o'er thy cheek warm with desire;
And carefully thou hast cherished thy white skin;
Not in the sun's swart beams, but in cool shade,
Wooing soft Aphrodite with thy loveliness.
But tell me first, from whence hath sprung thy race?

DIONYSUS   There needs no boast; 'tis easy to tell this:
             All flowery Tmolus hast thou haply heard?

PENTHEUS   Yea; that which girds around the Sardian city.

DIONYSUS   Thence am I come, my country Lydia.

PENTHEUS   Whence unto Hellas bringest thou thine orgies?

DIONYSUS   Dionysus, son of Jove, hath hallowed them.

PENTHEUS   Is there a Jove then, that begets new gods?

DIONYSUS   No, it was here he wedded Semele.

PENTHEUS   Hallowed he them by night, or in the eye of day?

DIONYSUS   In open vision he revealed his orgies.

PENTHEUS   And what, then, is thine orgies' solemn form;

DIONYSUS   That is not uttered to the uninitiate.

PENTHEUS   What profit, then, is theirs who worship him?

DIONYSUS   Thou mayst not know, though precious were that
             knowledge.

PENTHEUS   A cunning tale, to make me long to hear thee.

DIONYSUS   The orgies of our god scorn impious worshippers.

PENTHEUS   Thou saw'st the manifest god! What was his form?

DIONYSUS   Whate'er he would: it was not mine to choose.

PENTHEUS   Cleverly blinked our question with no answer.

DIONYSUS   Who wiseliest speaks, to the fool speaks foolishness.

PENTHEUS   And hither com'st thou first with thy new god!

DIONYSUS   There's no Barbarian but adores these rites.

PENTHEUS   Being much less wise than we Hellenians.

DIONYSUS   In this more wise. Their customs differ much.

PENTHEUS   Performest thou these rites by night or day?

DIONYSUS   Most part by night — night hath more solemn awe.

PENTHEUS   A crafty rotten plot to catch our women.

DIONYSUS   Even in the day bad men can do bad deeds.

PENTHEUS   Thou of thy wiles shalt pay the penalty.

DIONYSUS   Thou of thine ignorance — impious towards the gods!

PENTHEUS   He's bold, this Bacchus — ready enough in words.

DIONYSUS   What penalty? what evil wilt thou do me?

PENTHEUS   First will I clip away those soft bright locks.

DIONYSUS   My locks are holy, dedicate to my god.

PENTHEUS   Next, give thou me that thyrsus in thine hand.

DIONYSUS   Take it thyself; 'tis Dionysus' wand.

PENTHEUS   I'll bind thy body in strong iron chains.

DIONYSUS   My god himself will loose them when he will.

PENTHEUS   When thou invok'st him 'mid thy Bacchanals.

DIONYSUS   Even now he is present; he beholds me now.

PENTHEUS   Where is he then? Mine eyes perceive him not.

DIONYSUS   Near me: the impious eyes may not discern him.

PENTHEUS   Seize on him, for he doth insult our Thebes.

DIONYSUS   I warn thee, bind me not; the insane, the sane.

PENTHEUS   I, stronger than thou art, say I will bind thee.

DIONYSUS   Thou know'st not where thou art, or what thou art.

PENTHEUS   Pentheus, Agave's son, my sire Echion.

DIONYSUS   Thou hast a name whose very sound is woe.

PENTHEUS   Away, go bind him in our royal stable,
            That he may sit in midnight gloom profound
        There lead thy dance! But those thou hast hither led,
        Thy guilt's accomplices, we'll sell for slaves;
        Or, silencing their noise and beating drums,
        As handmaids to the distaff set them down.

DIONYSUS   Away then! 'Tis not well I bear such wrong;
        The vengeance for this outrage he will wreak
        Whose being thou deniest, Dionysus:
        Outraging me, ye bind him in your chains.

CHORUS   Holy virgin-haunted water
              Ancient Achelous' daughter!

Dirce! in thy crystal wave
Thou the child of Jove didst lave.
Thou, when Zeus, his awful sire,
Snatched him from the immortal fire;
And locked him up within his thigh,
With a loud but gentle cry —
"Come, my Dithyrambus, come,
Enter thou the masculine womb!"
   Lo! to Thebes I thus proclaim,
"Twice born!" thus thy mystic name.
Blessed Dirce! dost thou well
From thy green marge to repel
Me, and all my jocund round,
With their ivy garlands crowned.
     Why dost fly me?
     Why deny me?
By all the joys of wine I swear,
Bromius still shall be my care.

Oh, what pride! pride unforgiven
Manifests, against high heaven
Th' earth-born, whom in mortal birth
'Gat Echion, son of earth;
Pentheus of the dragon brood,
Not of human flesh and blood;
But potent dire, like him whose pride,
The Titan, all the gods defied.
Me, great Bromius' handmaid true;
Me, with all my festive crew,
Thralled in chains he still would keep
In his palace dungeon deep.

Seest thou this, O son of Jove,
Dionysus, from above?
Thy wrapt prophets dost thou see
At strife with dark necessity?
    The golden wand
    In thy right hand.
Come, come thou down Olympus' side,
And quell the bloody tyrant in his pride.·

Art thou holding revel now
On Nysa's wild beast-haunted brow?
Is't thy Thyasus that clambers
O'er Corycia's mountain chambers?
Or on Olympus, thick with wood,
With his harp where Orpheus stood,
And led the forest trees along,
Led the wild beasts with his song.
    O Pieria, blessed land,
Evius hallows thee, advancing,
With his wild choir's mystic dancing,
    Over rapid Axius' strand
He shall pass; o'er Lydia's tide
Then his whirling Mænads guide.
Lydia, parent boon of health,
Giver to man of boundless wealth;
Washing many a sunny mead,
Where the prancing coursers feed.

DIONYSUS   What ho! what ho! ye Bacchanals
Rouse and wake! your master calls.

CHORUS   Who is here? and what is he
      That calls upon our wandering train?

DIONYSUS What ho! what ho! I call again!
      The son of Jove and Semele.

CHORUS   What ho! what ho! our lord and master:
    Come, with footsteps fast and faster,
    Join our revel! Bromius, speed,
      Till quakes the earth beneath our tread.
        Alas! alas!
  Soon shall Pentheus' palace wall
  Shake and crumble to its fall.

DIONYSUS Bacchus treads the palace floor!
  Adore him!

CHORUS   Oh! we do adore!
        Behold! behold!
    The pillars with their weight above,
    Of ponderous marble, shake and move.
    Hark! the trembling roof within
    Bacchus shouts his mighty din.

DIONYSUS The kindling lamp of the dark lightning bring!
  Fire, fire the palace of the guilty king.

CHORUS Behold! behold! it flames! Do ye not see,
    Around the sacred tomb of Semele,
    The blaze, that left the lightning there,
    When Jove's red thunder fired the air?
      On the earth, supine and low,
      Your shuddering limbs, ye Mænads, throw!

The king, the Jove-born god, destroying all,
In widest ruin strews the palace wall.

DIONYSUS   O, ye Barbarian women, Thus prostrate in dismay;
Upon the earth ye've fallen! See ye not, as ye may,
How Bacchus Pentheus' palace In wrath hath shaken
down?
Rise up! rise up! take courage — Shake off that
trembling swoon.

CHORUS O light that goodliest shinest Over our mystic rite,
In state forlorn we saw thee — Saw with what deep
affright!

DIONYSUS   How to despair ye yielded As I boldly entered in
To Pentheus, as if captured, Into the fatal gin.

CHORUS How could I less? Who guards us If thou shouldst come
to woe?
But how wast thou delivered From thy ungodly foe?

DIONYSUS   Myself, myself delivered, With ease and effort slight.

CHORUS Thy hands, had he not bound them, In halters strong
and tight?

DIONYSUS   'Twas even then I mocked him: He thought me in his
chain;
He touched me not, nor reached me; His idle thoughts
were vain!
In the stable stood a heifer, Where he thought he had
me bound:
Round the beast's knees his cords And cloven hoofs he
wound.

Wrath-breathing, from his body The sweat fell like a flood:

He bit his lips in fury, While I beside who stood

Looked on in unmoved quiet.

                            As at that instant come,

Shook Bacchus the strong palace, And on his mother's tomb

Flames kindled. When he saw it, On fire the palace deeming,

Hither he rushed and thither, For "water, water," screaming;

And every slave 'gan labour, But laboured all in vain.

The toil he soon abandoned. As though I had fled amain

He rushed into the palace: In his hand the dark sword gleamed.

Then, as it seemed, great Bromius — I say, but as it seemed —

In the hall a bright light kindled. On that he rushed, and there,

As slaying me in vengeance, Stood stabbing the thin air.

But then the avenging Bacchus Wrought new calamities;

From roof to base that palace In smouldering ruin lies.

Bitter ruing our imprisonment, With toil forspent he threw

On earth his useless weapon. Mortal, he had dared to do

'Gainst a god unholy battle. But I, in quiet state,

Unheeding Pentheus' anger, Came through the palace
    gate.
It seems even now his sandal Is sounding on its way:
Soon is he here before us, And what now will he say?
With ease will I confront him, Ire-breathing though he
    stand.
'Tis easy to a wise man To practise self-command.

PENTHEUS   I am outraged — mocked! The stranger hath escaped
    me
Whom I so late had bound in iron chains.
Off, off! He is here! — the man? How's this? How stands
    he
Before our palace, as just issuing forth?

DIONYSUS   Stay thou thy step! Subdue thy wrath to peace!

PENTHEUS   How, having burst thy chains, hast thou come forth?

DIONYSUS   Said I not — heardst thou not? "There's one will free
    me!"

PENTHEUS   What one? Thou speakest still words new and
    strange.

DIONYSUS   He who for man plants the rich-tendrilled vine.

PENTHEUS   Well layest thou this reproach on Dionysus.
    Without there, close and bar the towers around!

DIONYSUS   What! and the gods! O'erleap they not all walls?

PENTHEUS   Wise in all wisdom save in that thou shouldst have!

DIONYSUS   In that I should have wisest still am I.

But listen first, and hear the words of him
Who comes to thee with tidings from the mountains
Here will we stay. Fear not, we will not fly!

MESSENGER   Pentheus, that rulest o'er this land of Thebes!
I come from high Cithæron, ever white
With the bright glittering snow's perennial rays.

PENTHEUS   Why com'st thou? On what pressing mission bound?

MESSENGER   I've seen the frenzied Bacchanals, who had fled
On their white feet, forth goaded from the land.
I come to tell to thee and to this city
The awful deeds they do, surpassing wonder.
But answer first if I shall freely say
All that's done there, or furl my prudent speech;
For thy quick temper I do fear, O king,
Thy sharp resentment and o'er-royal pride.

PENTHEUS   Speak freely. Thou shall part unharmed by me;
Wrath were not seemly 'gainst the unoffending.
But the more awful what thou sayst of these
Mad women, I the more on him who hath guiled
    them
To their wild life, will wreak my just revenge.

MESSENGER   Mine herds of heifers I was driving, slow
Winding their way along the mountain crags,
When the sun pours his full beams on the earth.
I saw three bands, three choirs of women: one
Autonoe led, thy mother led the second,
Agave — and the third Ino: and all
Quietly slept, their languid limbs stretched out:

Some resting on the ash-trees' stem their tresses;
Some with their heads upon the oak-leaves thrown
Careless, but not immodest; as thou sayest,
That drunken with the goblet and shrill fife
In the dusk woods they prowl for lawless love.
Thy mother, as she heard the hornéd steers
Deep lowing, stood up 'mid the Bacchanals
And shouted loud to wake them from their rest.
They from their lids shaking the freshening sleep,
Rose upright, wonderous in their decent guise,
The young, the old, the maiden yet unwed.
And first they loosed their locks over their shoulders,
Their fawn-skins fastened, wheresoe'er the clasps
Had lost their hold, and all the dappled furs
With serpents bound, that lolled out their lithe tongues.
Some in their arms held kid, or wild-wolf's cub,
Suckling it with her white milk; all the young mothers
Who had left their new-born babes, and stood with
         breasts
Full swelling: and they all put on their crowns
Of ivy, oak, or flowering eglantine.
One took a thyrsus wand, and struck the rock,
Leaped forth at once a dewy mist of water;
And one her rod plunged deep in the earth, and there
The god sent up a fountain of bright wine.
And all that longed for the white blameless draught
Light scraping with their finger-ends the soil
Had streams of exquisite milk; the ivy wands
Distilled from all their tops rich store of honey.
   Hadst thou been there, seeing these things, the god
Thou now revil'st thou hadst adored with prayer.

And we, herdsmen and shepherds, gathered around
And there was strife among us in our words
Of these strange things they did, these marvellous
     things.
One city-bred, a glib and practised speaker,
Addressed us thus: "Ye that inhabit here
The holy mountain slopes, shall we not chase
Agave, Pentheus' mother, from the Bacchanals,
And win the royal favour?" Well to us
He seemed to speak; so, crouched in the thick bushes,
We lay in ambush. They at the appointed hour
Shook their wild thyrsi in the Bacchic dance,
"Iacchus" with one voice, the son of Jove,
"Bromius" invoking. The hills danced with them;
And the wild beasts; was nothing stood unmoved.
     And I leaped forth, as though to seize on her,
Leaving the sedge where I had hidden myself.
But she shrieked out, "Ho, my swift-footed dogs!
These men would hunt us down, but follow me —
Follow me, all your hands with thyrsi armed."
We fled amain, or by the Bacchanals
We had been torn in pieces. They, with hands
Unarmed with iron, rushed on the browsing steers.
One ye might see a young and vigorous heifer
Hold, lowing in her grasp, like prize of war.
And some were tearing asunder the young calves;
And ye might see the ribs or cloven hoofs
Hurled wildly up and down, and mangled skins
Were hanging from the ash boughs, dropping blood.
The wanton bulls, proud of their tossing horns
Of yore, fell stumbling, staggering to the ground,

Dragged down by the strong hands of thousand
    maidens.
And swifter were the entrails torn away
Than drop the lids over your royal eyeballs.
    Like birds that skim the earth, they glide along
O'er the wide plains, that by Asopus' streams
Shoot up for Thebes the rich and yellow corn;
And Hysiæ and Erythræ, that beneath
Cithæron's crag dwell lowly, like fierce foes
Invading, all with ravage waste and wide
Confounded; infants snatched from their sweet homes;
And what they threw across their shoulders, clung
Unfastened, nor fell down to the black ground.
No brass, nor ponderous iron: on their locks
Was fire that burned them not. Of those they spoiled
Some in their sudden fury rushed to arms.
Then was a mightier wonder seen, O king:
From them the pointed lances drew no blood
But they their thyrsi hurling, javelin-like,
Drave all before, and smote their shameful backs:
Women drave men, but not without the god.
    So did they straight return from whence they came,
Even to the fountains, which the god made flow;
Washed off the blood, and from their cheeks the drops
The serpents licked, and made them bright and clean.
This godhead then, whoe'er he be, my master!
Receive within our city. Great in all things,
In this I hear men say he is the greatest —
He hath given the sorrow-soothing vine to man
For where wine is not love will never be,
Nor any other joy of human life.

CHORUS I am afraid to speak the words of freedom
              Before the tyrant, yet it must be said:
              "Inferior to no god is Dionysus."

PENTHEUS 'Tis here then, like a wild fire, burning on,
                This Bacchic insolence, Hellas' deep disgrace.
                Off with delay! Go to the Electrian gates
                And summon all that bear the shield, and all
                The cavalry upon their prancing steeds,
                And those that couch the lance, and of the bow
                Twang the sharp string. Against these Bacchanals
                We will go war. It were indeed too much
                From women to endure what we endure.

DIONYSUS Thou wilt not be persuaded by my words
                Pentheus! Yet though of thee I have suffered wrong
                I warn thee, rise not up against the god.
                Rest thou in peace. Bromius will never brook
                Ye drive his Mænads from their mountain haunts.

PENTHEUS Wilt teach me? Better fly and save thyself,
                Ere yet I wreak stern justice upon thee.

DIONYSUS Rather do sacrifice, than in thy wrath
                Kick 'gainst the pricks — a mortal 'gainst a god.

PENTHEUS I'll sacrifice, and in Cithæron's glens,
                As they deserve, a hecatomb of women.

DIONYSUS Soon will ye fly. 'Twere shame that shields of brass
                Before the Bacchic thyrsi turn in rout.

PENTHEUS   I am bewildered by this dubious stranger;
        Doing or suffering, he holds not his peace.

DIONYSUS   My friend! Thou still mayest bring this to good end.

PENTHEUS   How so? By being the slave of mine own slaves?

DIONYSUS   These women — without force of arms, I'll bring
        them.

PENTHEUS   Alas! he is plotting now some wile against me!

DIONYSUS   But what if I could save thee by mine arts?

PENTHEUS   Ye are all in league, that ye may hold your orgies.

DIONYSUS   I am in a league 'tis true, but with the god!

PENTHEUS   Bring out mine armour! Thou, have done thy
        speech!

DIONYSUS   Ha! wouldst thou see them seated on the mountains?

PENTHEUS   Ay! for the sight give thousand weight of gold.

DIONYSUS   Why hast thou fallen upon this strange desire?

PENTHEUS   'Twere grief to see them in their drunkenness.

DIONYSUS   Yet gladly wouldst thou see, what see would grieve
        thee.

PENTHEUS   Mark well! in silence seated 'neath the ash-trees.

DIONYSUS   But if thou goest in secret they will scent thee.

PENTHEUS   Best openly, in this thou hast said well.

DIONYSUS   But if we lead thee, wilt thou dare the way?

PENTHEUS   Lead on, and swiftly! Let no time be lost!

DIONYSUS   But first enwrap thee in these linen robes.

PENTHEUS   What, will he of a man make me a woman!

DIONYSUS   Lest they should kill thee, seeing thee as a man.

PENTHEUS   Well dost thou speak; so spake the wise of old.

DIONYSUS   Dionysus hath instructed me in this.

PENTHEUS   How then can we best do what thou advisest?

DIONYSUS   I'll enter in the house, and there array thee.

PENTHEUS   What dress? A woman's? I am ashamed to wear it.

DIONYSUS   Art thou not eager to behold the Mænads?

PENTHEUS   And what dress sayst thou I must wrap around me?

DIONYSUS   I'll smooth thine hair down lightly on thy brow.

PENTHEUS   What is the second portion of my dress?

DIONYSUS   Robes to thy feet, a bonnet on thine head.

PENTHEUS   Wilt thou array me then in more than this?

DIONYSUS   A thyrsus in thy hand, a dappled fawn-skin.

PENTHEUS   I cannot clothe me in a woman's dress.

DIONYSUS   Thou wilt have bloodshed, warring on the Mænads.

PENTHEUS   'Tis right, I must go first survey the field.

DIONYSUS   'Twere wiser than to hunt evil with evil.

PENTHEUS   How pass the city, unseen of the Thebans?

DIONYSUS   We'll go by lone byways; I'll lead thee safe.

PENTHEUS   Aught better than be mocked by these loose
                 Bacchanals.
            When we come back, we'll counsel what were best.

DIONYSUS   Even as you will: I am here at your command.

PENTHEUS   'So let us on; I must go forth in arms,
            Or follow the advice thou givest me.

DIONYSUS   Women! this man is in our net; he goes
            To find his just doom 'mid the Bacchanals.
            Dionysus, to thy work! thou'rt not far off;
            Vengeance is ours. Bereave him first of sense:
            Yet be his frenzy slight. In his right mind
            He never had put on a woman's dress;
            But now, thus shaken in his mind, he'll wear it.
            A laughing-stock I'll make him to all Thebes,
            Led in a woman's dress through the wide city.
            For those fierce threats in which he was so great.
            But I must go, and Pentheus — in the garb
            Which wearing, even by his own mother's hand
            Slain, he goes down to Hades. Know he must
            Dionysus, son of Jove, among the gods
            Mightiest, yet mildest to the sons of men.

CHORUS   O when, through the long night,
                With fleet foot glancing white,

Shall I go dancing in my revelry,
    My neck cast back, and bare
    Unto the dewy air,
Like sportive fawn in the green meadow's glee?
    Lo, in her fear she springs
    Over th' encircling rings,
Over the well-woven nets far off and fast;
    While swift along her track
    The huntsman cheers his pack,
With panting toil, and fiery storm-wind haste.
Where down the river-bank spreads the wide meadow
    Rejoices she in the untrod solitude.
Couches at length beneath the silent shadow
    Of the old hospitable wood.

    What is wisest? what is fairest,
    Of god's boons to man the rarest?
    With the conscious conquering hand
    Above the foeman's head to stand.
    What is fairest still is dearest.

    Slow come, but come at length,
    In their majestic strength
Faithful and true, the avenging deities:
    And chastening human folly,
    And the mad pride unholy,
Of those who to the gods bow not their knees.
    For hidden still and mute,
    As glides their printless foot,
The impious on their winding path they hound
    For it is ill to know,
    And it is ill to do,

Beyond the law's inexorable bound.
'Tis but light cost in his own power sublime
    To array the godhead, whosoe'er he be;
And law is old, even as the oldest time,
    Nature's own unrepealed decree.

    What is wisest? what is fairest,
    Of god's boons to man the rarest?
    With the conscious conquering hand
    Above the foeman's head to stand
    What is fairest still is rarest.

    Who hath 'scaped the turbulent sea,
    And reached the haven, happy he!
    Happy he whose toils are o'er,
    In the race of wealth and power!
    This one here, and that one there,
    Passes by, and everywhere
    Still expectant thousands over
    Thousands hopes are seen to hover,
    Some to mortals end in bliss;
    Some have already fled away:
    Happiness alone is his
    That happy is to-day.

DIONYSUS   Thou art mad to see that which thou shouldst not see,
    And covetous of that thou shouldst not covet.
    Pentheus! I say, come forth! Appear before me,
    Clothed in the Bacchic Mænads' womanly dress;
    Spy on thy mother and her holy crew,
    Come like in form to one of Cadmus' daughters.

PENTHEUS   Ha! now indeed two suns I seem to see,
                       A double Thebes, two seven-gated cities;
                       Thou, as a bull, seemest to go before me,
                       And horns have grown upon thine head. Art thou
                       A beast indeed? Thou seem'st a very bull.

DIONYSUS   The god is with us; unpropitious once,
                       But now at truce: now seest thou what thou shouldst see?

PENTHEUS   What see I? Is not that the step of Ino?
                       And is not Agave there, my mother?

DIONYSUS   Methinks 'tis even they whom thou behold'st;
                       But lo! this tress hath strayed out of its place,
                       Not as I braided it, beneath thy bonnet.

PENTHEUS   Tossing it this way now, now tossing that,
                       In Bacchic glee, I have shaken it from its place.

DIONYSUS   But we, whose charge it is to watch o'er thee,
                       Will braid it up again. Lift up thy head.

PENTHEUS   Braid as thou wilt, we yield ourselves to thee.

DIONYSUS   Thy zone is loosened, and thy robe's long folds
                       Droop outward, nor conceal thine ankles now.

PENTHEUS   Around my right foot so it seems, yet sure
                       Around the other it sits close and well.

DIONYSUS   Wilt thou not hold me for thy best of friends,
                       Thus strangely seeing the coy Bacchanals?

PENTHEUS   The thyrsus — in my right hand shall I hold it?
                       Or thus am I more like a Bacchanal?

DIONYSUS   In thy right hand, and with thy right foot raise it.
            I praise the change of mind now come o'er thee.

PENTHEUS   Could I not now bear up upon my shoulders
            Cithæron's crag, with all the Bacchanals?

DIONYSUS   Thou couldst if 'twere thy will. In thy right mind
            Erewhile thou wast not; now thou art as thou shouldst
            be.

PENTHEUS   Shall I take levers, pluck it up with my hands,
            Or thrust mine arm or shoulder 'neath its base?

DIONYSUS   Destroy thou not the dwellings of the nymphs,
            The seats where Pan sits piping in his joy.

PENTHEUS   Well hast thou said; by force we conquer not
            These women. I'll go hide in yonder ash.

DIONYSUS   Within a fatal ambush wilt thou hide thee,
            Stealing, a treacherous spy, upon the Mænads.

PENTHEUS   And now I seem to see them there like birds
            Couching on their soft beds amid the fern.

DIONYSUS   Art thou not therefore set as watchman o'er them?
            Thou'lt seize them — if they do not seize thee first.

PENTHEUS   Lead me triumphant through the land of Thebes!
            I, only I, have dared a deed like this.

DIONYSUS   Thou art the city's champion, thou alone.
            Therefore a strife thou wot'st not of awaits thee.

Follow me! thy preserver goes before thee;
Another takes thee hence.

PENTHEUS   Mean'st thou my mother?

DIONYSUS   Aloft shalt thou be borne.

PENTHEUS   O the soft carriage!

DIONYSUS   In thy mother's hands.

PENTHEUS   Wilt make me thus luxurious?

DIONYSUS   Strange luxury, indeed!

PENTHEUS   'Tis my desert.

DIONYSUS   Thou art awful! — awful! Doomed to awful end!
          Thy glory shall soar up to the high heavens!
             Stretch forth thine hand, Agave! — ye her kin,
          Daughters of Cadmus! To a terrible grave
          Lead I this youth! Myself shall win the prize —
          Bromius and I; the event will show the rest.

CHORUS Ho! fleet dogs and furious, to the mountains, ho!
          Where their mystic revels Cadmus' daughters keep.
             Rouse them, goad them out,
          'Gainst him, in woman's mimic garb concealed,
          Gazer on the Mænads in their dark rites unrevealed.
          First his mother shall behold him on his watch below,
          From the tall tree's trunk or from the wild scaur steep;
                  Fiercely will she shout —
          "Who the spy upon the Mænads on the rocks that roam

To the mountain, to the mountain, Bacchanals, has
    come?"
                     Who hath borne him?

      He is not of woman's blood —
           The lioness!
       Or the Lybian Gorgon's brood?
    Come, vengeance, come, display thee!
    With thy bright sword array thee!
       The bloody sentence wreak
        On the dissevered neck
Of him who god, law, justice hath not known,
      Echion's earth-born son.

He, with thought unrighteous and unholy pride,
'Gainst Bacchus and his mother, their orgies' mystic
    mirth
      Still holds his frantic strife,
And sets him up against the god, deeming it light
      To vanquish the invincible of might.
Hold thou fast the pious mind; so, only so, shall glide
In peace with gods above, in peace with men on earth,
      Thy smooth painless life.
I admire not, envy not, who would be otherwise:
Mine be still the glory, mine be still the prize,
        By night and day
      To live of the immortal gods in awe;
       Who fears them not
      Is but the outcast of all law.

    Come, vengeance, come display thee!
    With thy bright sword array thee!

> The bloody sentence wreak
> On the dissevered neck
> Of him who god, law, justice has not known,
> Echion's earth-born son.
>
> Appear! appear!
> Or as the stately steer!
> Or many-headed dragon be!
> Or the fire-breathing lion, terrible to see.
> Come, Bacchus, come 'gainst the hunter of the
> Bacchanals,
> Even now, now as he falls
> Upon the Mænads' fatal herd beneath,
> With smiling brow,
> Around him throw
> The inexorable net of death.

MESSENGER O house most prosperous once throughout all
Hellas!
House of the old Sidonian! — in this land
Who sowed the dragon's serpent's earth-born harvest —
How I deplore thee! I a slave, for still
Grieve for their master's sorrows faithful slaves.

CHORUS What's this? Aught new about the Bacchanals?

MESSENGER   Pentheus hath perished, old Echion's son.

CHORUS King Bromius, thou art indeed a mighty god!

MESSENGER   What sayst thou? How is this? Rejoicest thou,
O woman, in my master's awful fate?

CHORUS Light chants the stranger her barbarous strains;
       I cower not in fear for the menace of chains.

MESSENGER   All Thebes thus void of courage deemest thou?

CHORUS O Dionysus! Dionysus! Thebes
       Hath o'er me now no power.

MESSENGER   'Tis pardonable, yet it is not well,
       Woman, in others' miseries to rejoice.

CHORUS Tell me, then, by what fate died the unjust —
       The man, the dark contriver of injustice?

MESSENGER   Therapnæ having left the Theban city,
       And passed along Asopus' winding shore,
       We 'gan to climb Cithæron's upward steep —
       Pentheus and I (I waited on my lord),
       And he that led us on our quest, the stranger —
       And first we crept along a grassy glade,
       With silent footsteps, and with silent tongues
       Slow moving, as to see, not being seen.
       There was a rock-walled glen, watered by a streamlet,
       And shadowed o'er with pines; the Mænads there
       Sate, all their hands busy with pleasant toil;
       And some the leafy thyrsus, that its ivy
       Had dropped away, were garlanding anew;
       Like fillies some, unharnessed from the yoke;
       Chanted alternate all the Bacchic hymn.
       Ill-fated Pentheus, as he scarce could see
       That womanly troop, spake thus: "Where we stand, stranger,

We see not well the unseemly Mænad dance:
But, mounting on a bank, or a tall tree,
Clearly shall I behold their deeds of shame."
    A wonder then I saw that stranger do.
He seized an ash-tree's high heaven-reaching stem,
And dragged it down, dragged, dragged to the low earth;
And like a bow it bent. As a curved wheel
Becomes a circle in the turner's lathe,
The stranger thus that mountain tree bent down
To the earth, a deed of more than mortal strength.
Then seating Pentheus on those ash-tree boughs,
Upward he let it rise, steadily, gently
Through his hands, careful lest it shake him off;
And slowly rose it upright to its height,
Bearing my master seated on its ridge.
There was he seen, rather than saw the Mænads,
More visible he could not be, seated aloft.
The stranger from our view had vanished quite.
Then from the heavens a voice, as it should seem
Dionysus, shouted loud, "Behold! I bring,
O maidens, him that you and me, our rites,
Our orgies laughed to scorn; now take your vengeance."
And as he spake, a light of holy fire
Stood up, and blazed from earth straight up to heaven.
Silent the air, silent the verdant grove
Held its still leaves; no sound of living thing.
They, as their ears just caught the half-heard voice,
Stood up erect, and rolled their wondering eyes.
Again he shouted. But when Cadmus' daughters
Heard manifest the god's awakening voice,

Forth rushed they, fleeter than the wingéd dove,
Their nimble feet quick coursing up and down.
Agave first, his mother, then her kin,
The Mænads, down the torrents' bed, in the grove,
From crag to crag they leaped, mad with the god.
And first with heavy stones they hurled at him,
Climbing a rock in front; the branches some
Of the ash-tree darted; some like javelins
Sent their sharp thyrsi through the sounding air,
Pentheus their mark: but yet they struck him not;
His height still baffled all their eager wrath.
There sat the wretch, helpless in his despair.
The oaken boughs, by lightning as struck off,
Roots torn from the earth, but with no iron wedge,
They hurled, but their wild labours all were vain.
Agave spake, "Come all, and stand around,
And grasp the tree, ye Mænads; soon we will seize
The beast that rides thereon. He will ne'er betray
The mysteries of our god." A thousand hands
Were on the ash, and tore it from the earth:
And he that sat aloft, down, headlong, down
Fell to the ground, with thousand piteous shrieks,
Pentheus, for well he knew his end was near.
His mother first began the sacrifice,
And fell on him. His bonnet from his hair
He threw, that she might know and so not slay him,
The sad Agave. And he said, her cheek
Fondling, "I am thy child, thine own, my mother!
Pentheus, whom in Echion's house you bare.
Have mercy on me, mother! For his sins,

Whatever be his sins, kill not thy son."
She, foaming at the mouth, her rolling eyeballs
Whirling around, in her unreasoning reason,
By Bacchus all possessed, knew, heeded not.
She caught him in her arms, seized his right hand,
And, with her feet set on his shrinking side,
Tore out the shoulder — not with her own strength:
The god made easy that too cruel deed.
And Ino laboured on the other side,
Rending the flesh: Autonoe, all the rest,
Pressed fiercely on, and there was one wild din —
He groaning deep, while he had breath to groan,
They shouting triumph; and one bore an arm,
One a still-sandalled foot; and both his sides
Lay open, rent. Each in her bloody hand
Tossed wildly to and fro lost Pentheus' limbs.
The trunk lay far aloof, 'neath the rough rocks
Part, part amid the forest's thick-strewn leaves
Not easy to be found. The wretched head,
Which the mad mother, seizing in her hands
Had on a thyrsus fixed, she bore aloft
All o'er Cithæron, as a mountain lion's,
Leading her sisters in their Mænad dance.
And she comes vaunting her ill-fated chase
Unto these walls, invoking Bacchus still,
Her fellow-hunter, partner in her prey,
Her triumph — triumph soon to end in tears!
I fled the sight of that dark tragedy,
Hastening, ere yet Agave reached the palace.
Oh! to be reverent, to adore the gods,

This is the noblest, wisest course of man,
Taking dread warning from this dire event.

CHORUS   Dance and sing
                        In Bacchic ring,
        Shout, shout the fate, the fate of gloom,
            Of Pentheus, from the dragon born;
            He the woman's garb hath worn,
Following the bull, the harbinger, that led him to his doom.
            O ye Theban Bacchanals!
        Attune ye now the hymn victorious,
            The hymn all glorious,
        To the tear, and to the groan!
            Oh game of glory!
        To bathe the hands besprent and gory,
            In the blood of her own son.
        But I behold Agave, Pentheus' mother,
        Nearing the palace with distorted eyes.
        Hail we the ovation of the Evian god.

AGAVE   O ye Asian Bacchanals!

CHORUS   Who is she on us who calls?

AGAVE   From the mountains, lo! we bear
                    To the palace gate
                Our new-slain quarry fair.

CHORUS   I see, I see! and on thy joy I wait.

AGAVE   Without a net, without a snare,
            The lion's cub, I took him there

CHORUS   In the wilderness, or where?

AGAVE   Cithæron —

CHORUS   Of Cithæron what?

AGAVE   Gave him to slaughter.

CHORUS   O blest Agave!

AGAVE   In thy song extol me,

CHORUS   Who struck him first?

AGAVE   Mine, mine, the glorious lot.

CHORUS   Who else?

AGAVE   Of Cadmus —

CHORUS   What of Cadmus' daughter?

AGAVE   With me, with me, did all the race
             Hound the prey.

CHORUS   O fortunate chase!

AGAVE   The banquet share with me!

CHORUS   Alas! what shall our banquet be?

AGAVE   How delicate the kid and young!
             The thin locks have but newly sprung
             Over his forehead fair.

CHORUS 'Tis beauteous as the tame beasts' cherished hair.

AGAVE   Bacchus, hunter known to fame!
             Did he not our Mænads bring

On the track of this proud game?
    A mighty hunter is our king!
Praise me! praise me!

CHORUS   Praise I not thee?

AGAVE   Soon with the Thebans all, the hymn of praise
Pentheus my son will to his mother raise:
    For she the lion prey hath won,
    A noble deed and nobly done.

CHORUS   Dost thou rejoice?

AGAVE   Ay, with exulting voice
My great, great deed I elevate,
        Glorious as great.

CHORUS Sad woman, to the citizens of Thebes
Now show the conquered prey thou bearest hither.

AGAVE   Ye that within the high-towered Theban city
Dwell, come and gaze ye all upon our prey,
The mighty beast by Cadmus' daughter ta'en;
Nor with Thessalian sharp-pointed javelins,
Nor nets, but with the white and delicate palms
Of our own hands. Go ye, and make your boast,
Trusting to the spear-maker's useless craft:
We with these hands have ta'en our prey, and rent
The mangled limbs of this grim beast asunder.
    Where is mine aged sire? Let him draw near!
And where is my son Pentheus? Let him mount
On the broad stairs that rise before our house;
And on the triglyph nail this lion's head,
That I have brought him from our splendid chase.

CADMUS   Follow me, follow, bearing your sad burthen,
          My servants — Pentheus' body — to our house;
          The body that with long and weary search
          I found at length in lone Cithæron's glens;
          Thus torn, not lying in one place, but wide
          Scattered amid the dark and tangled thicket.
          Already, as I entered in the city
          With old Tiresias, from the Bacchanals,
          I heard the fearful doings of my daughter.
          And back returning to the mountain, bear
          My son, thus by the furious Mænads slain.
          Her who Actæon bore to Aristæus,
          Autonoë, I saw, and Ino with her
          Still in the thicket goaded with wild madness.
          And some one said that on her dancing feet
          Agave had come hither — true he spoke;
          I see her now — O most unblessed sight!

AGAVE   Father, 'tis thy peculiar peerless boast
          Of womanhood the noblest t' have begot —
          Me — me the noblest of that noble kin.
          For I the shuttle and the distaff left
          For mightier deeds — wild beasts with mine own hands
          To capture. Lo! I bear within mine arms
          These glorious trophies, to be hung on high
          Upon thy house: receive them, O my father!
          Call thy friends to the banquet feast! Blest thou!
          Most blest, through us who have wrought such splendid
                deeds.

CADMUS   Measureless grief! Eye may not gaze on it,
          The slaughter wrought by those most wretched hands.

Oh! what a sacrifice before the gods!
All Thebes, and us, thou callest to the feast.
Justly — too justly, hath King Bromius
Destroyed us, fatal kindred to our house.

AGAVE   Oh! how morose is man in his old age,
And sullen in his mien. Oh! were my son
More like his mother, mighty in his hunting,
When he goes forth among the youth of Thebes
Wild beasts to chase! But he is great alone,
In warring on the gods. We two, my sire,
Must counsel him against his evil wisdom.
Where is he? Who will call him here before us
That he may see me in my happiness?

CADMUS Woe! woe! When ye have sense of what ye have done,
With what deep sorrow, sorrow ye! To th' end,
Oh! could ye be, only as now ye are,
Nor happy were ye deemed, nor miserable.

AGAVE   What is not well? For sorrow what the cause?

CADMUS First lift thine eyes up to the air around.

AGAVE   Behold! Why thus commandest me to gaze?

CADMUS Is all the same? Appears there not a change?

AGAVE   'Tis brighter, more translucent than before.

CADMUS Is there the same elation in thy soul?

AGAVE　　I know not what thou mean'st; but I become
　　　　　Conscious — my changing mind is settling down.

CADMUS　Canst thou attend, and plainly answer me?

AGAVE　　I have forgotten, father, all I said.

CADMUS　Unto whose bed wert thou in wedlock given?

AGAVE　　Echion's, him they call the Dragon-born.

CADMUS　Who was the son to thy husband thou didst bear?

AGAVE　　Pentheus, in commerce 'twixt his sire and me.

CADMUS　And whose the head thou holdest in thy hands?

AGAVE　　A lion's; thus my fellow-hunters said.

CADMUS　Look at it straight: to look on't is no toil.

AGAVE　　What see I? Ha! what's this within my hands?

CADMUS　Look on't again, again: thou wilt know too well.

AGAVE　　I see the direst woe that eye may see.

CADMUS　The semblance of a lion bears it now?

AGAVE　　No: wretch, wretch that I am; 'tis Pentheus' head!

CADMUS　Even ere yet recognised thou might'st have mourned
　　　　　him.

AGAVE　　Who murdered him? How came he in my hands?

CADMUS　Sad truth! Untimely dost thou ever come!

AGAVE   Speak; for my heart leaps with a boding throb.

CADMUS   'Twas thou didst slay him, thou and thine own sisters.

AGAVE   Where died he? In his palace? In what place?

CADMUS   There where the dogs Actæon tore in pieces.

AGAVE   Why to Cithæron went the ill-fated man?

CADMUS   To mock the god, to mock the orgies there.

AGAVE   But how and wherefore had we thither gone?

CADMUS   In madness! — the whole city maddened with thee.

AGAVE   Dionysus hath destroyed us! Late I learn it.

CADMUS   Mocked with dread mockery; no god ye held him.

AGAVE   Father! Where's the dear body of my son?

CADMUS   I bear it here, not found without much toil,

AGAVE   Are all the limbs together, sound and whole?
          And Pentheus, shared he in my desperate fury?

CADMUS   Like thee he was, he worshipped not the god.
          All, therefore, are enwrapt in one dread doom.
          You, he, in whom hath perished all our house,
          And I who, childless of male offspring, see
          This single fruit — O miserable! — of thy womb
          Thus shamefully, thus lamentably dead —
          Thy son, to whom our house looked up, the stay
          Of all our palace he, my daughter's son,

The awe of the whole city: None would dare
Insult the old man when thy fearful face
He saw, well knowing he would pay the penalty.
Unhonoured now, I am driven from out mine home;
Cadmus the great, who all the race of Thebes
Sowed in the earth, and reaped that harvest fair.
O best beloved of men, thou art now no more,
Yet still art dearest of my children thou!
No more, this grey beard fondling with thine hand,
Wilt call me thine own grandsire, thou sweet child,
And fold me round and say, "Who doth not honour
      thee?
Old man, who troubles or afflicts thine heart?
Tell me, that I may 'venge thy wrong, my father!"
Now wretchedst of men am I. Thou pitiable —
More pitiable thy mother — sad thy kin.
O if there be who scorneth the great gods,
Gaze on this death, and know that there are gods.

CHORUS   Cadmus, I grieve for thee. Thy daughter's son
         Hath his just doom — just, but most piteous.

AGAVE   Father, thou seest how all is changed with me:
         I am no more the Mænad dancing blithe,
         I am but the feeble, fond, and desolate mother.
         I know, I see — ah, knowledge best unknown!
         Sight best unseen! — I see, I know my son,
         Mine only son! — alas! no more my son.
         O beauteous limbs, that in my womb I bare!
         O head, that on my lap wast wont to sleep!
         O lips, that from my bosom's swelling fount
         Drained the delicious and soft-oozing milk!

O hands, whose first use was to fondle me!
O feet, that were so light to run to me!
O gracious form, that men wondering beheld!
O haughty brow, before which Thebes bowed down!
O majesty! O strength! by mine own hands —
By mine own murderous, sacrilegious hands —
Torn, rent asunder, scattered, cast abroad!
O thou hard god! was there no other way
To visit us? Oh! if the son must die,
Must it be by the hand of his own mother?
If the impious mother must atone her sin,
Must it be but by murdering her own son?

DIONYSUS   Now hear ye all, Thebes' founders, what is woven
By the dread shuttle of the unerring Fates.
Thou, Cadmus, father of this earth-born race,
A dragon shalt become; thy wife shalt take
A brutish form, and sink into a serpent,
Harmonia, Ares' daughter, whom thou wedd'st,
Though mortal, as Jove's oracle declares.
Thou in a car by heifers drawn shalt ride,
And with thy wife, at the Barbarians' head:
And many cities with their countless host
Shall they destroy, but when they dare destroy
The shrine of Loxias, back shall they return
In shameful flight; but Ares guards Harmonia
And thee, and bears you to the Isles of the Blest.
    This say I, of no mortal father born,
Dionysus, son of Jove. Had ye but known
To have been pious when ye might, Jove's son
Had been your friend; ye had been happy still.

AGAVE   Dionysus, we implore thee! We have sinned!

DIONYSUS   Too late ye say so; when ye should, ye would not.

AGAVE   That know we now; but thou'rt extreme in vengeance.

DIONYSUS   Was I not outraged, being a god, by you?

AGAVE   The gods should not be like to men in wrath.

DIONYSUS   This Jove, my father, long hath granted me.

AGAVE   Alas, old man! Our exile is decreed.

DIONYSUS   Why then delay ye the inevitable?

CADMUS   O child, to what a depth of woe we have fallen!
Most wretched thou, and all thy kin beloved!
I too to the Barbarians must depart,
An aged denizen. For there's a prophecy,
'Gainst Hellas a Barbaric mingled host
Harmonia leads, my wife, daughter of Ares.
A dragon I, with dragon nature fierce,
Shall lead the stranger spearmen 'gainst the altars
And tombs of Hellas, nor shall cease my woes —
Sad wretch! — not even when I have ferried o'er
Dark Acheron, shall I repose in peace.

AGAVE   Father! to exile go I without thee?

CADMUS   Why dost thou clasp me in thine arms, sad child,
A drone among the bees, a swan worn out?

AGAVE   Where shall I go, an exile from my country?

CADMUS   I know not, child; thy sire is a feeble aid.

AGAVE   Farewell, mine home! Farewell, my native Thebes!
         My bridal chamber! Banished, I go forth.

CADMUS   To the house of Aristæus go, my child.

AGAVE   I wait for thee, my father!

CADMUS   I for thee!
         And for thy sisters.

AGAVE   Fearfully, fearfully, this deep disgrace,
         Hath Dionysus brought upon our race.

DIONYSUS   Fearful on me the wrong that ye had done;
         Unhonoured was my name in Thebes alone.

AGAVE   Father, farewell!

CADMUS   Farewell, my wretched daughter!

AGAVE   So lead me forth — my sisters now to meet,
         Sad fallen exiles.
                        Let me, let me go
         Where cursed Cithæron ne'er may see me more,
         Nor I the cursed Cithæron see again.
         Where there's no memory of the thyrsus dance.
         The Bacchic orgies be the care of others.